CHRIS MARTIN BIOGRAPHY:

"Unveiling the Voice Behind Coldplay - From Exeter to World Fame"

CW01498773

Jaime S. Walker

TABLE OF CONTENTS

CHAPTER 1: INTRODUCTION

In addition to being a musician, Chris Martin, the main singer of *Coldplay*, is a visionary renowned for his poignant lyrics and distinctive sound. Chris was born in Exeter, England, on March 2, 1977.

His story of rising from a tiny village to global renown is motivational. He was the driving force behind *Coldplay* and contributed to the creation of some of the greatest singles of the past 20 years, including "Yellow," "Fix You," and "Viva La Vida." Beyond just his music, though, Chris is renowned for his commitment to global equality and environmental sustainability.

We'll explore Chris Martin's life narrative in this biography, from his early passion for music to *Coldplay*'s global success. We'll look at his personal biography, artistic development, and guiding principles. Learn how he became a voice for change and a global music icon.

CHAPTER 2: EARLY LIFE

On March 2, 1977, Chris Martin was born in Exeter, England. He was raised in a loving, musically inclined family as the eldest of five children. His mother, Alison, taught music, while his father, Anthony, worked as an accountant.

Chris's love of singing and playing instruments was profoundly inspired by this early musical exposure. Prior to joining the esteemed Sherborne School, Chris was a student at the Hylton School. From an early age, his love of music was apparent, and he frequently took part in school music festivals and events. Chris prepared for his future profession by taking piano and guitar lessons, which his parents helped fund.

Throughout his adolescence, his passion for music deepened, leading him to write songs and perform in local bands. These early experiences shaped his musical approach and prepared him for the challenges and pleasures that lay ahead.

2a. Early musical interests

Chris Martin's early musical tastes were impacted by the range of sounds he heard at home and at school. He was introduced to classical music and encouraged to take piano lessons by his mother, a music educator. Chris's classical training has given him a strong grasp of composition and music theory.

As Chris grew older, he developed a deep appreciation for rock and pop music. He was especially influenced by the bands U2, Radiohead, and The Beatles. The heartfelt lyrics, unique sounds, and wide variety of emotions exhibited by these performers moved him. Chris started writing his own songs, combining the classical techniques he had studied with his love of contemporary rock.

Chris Martin Biography..

Chris showed off his early flair for performance and songwriting when he created his first band, The Rocking Honkies, while attending Sherborne School. His confidence as a performer and sense of musical identity were greatly shaped during this time. The sound and success of Coldplay would ultimately be shaped by these early encounters and inspirations.

CHAPTER 3: UNIVERSITY YEARS

A major turning point in Chris Martin's life and career occurred during his undergraduate years. He began studying Ancient World Studies at University College London (UCL) in 1996. Here, in the midst of London's bustle, Chris would meet Coldplay's future bandmates and begin his journey to fame.

Chris first got to know musician Jonny Buckland during UCL's orientation week. Because they both loved music, they made the decision to start a band right away. Bassist Guy Berryman and drummer Will Champion soon completed the quartet. The trio decided to go with "Coldplay" instead of their previous alias, "Starfish," when a mutual friend suggested it.

The bandmates put in a lot of hours developing songs, practicing, and playing at local venues while juggling their education. When their debut EP, "Safety," was published in 1998, their diligence paid off. They gained recognition and a tiny but devoted following thanks to the EP.

Chris saw significant artistic growth during his time at university, in addition to academic pursuits. He improved as a songwriter, acquired a unique singing technique, and made enduring friendships that would influence his future. These college years cemented Chris Martin's career as a musician and prepared the way for Coldplay's ascent to prominence.

CHAPTER 4: FORMATION OF COLDPLAY

Coldplay was founded when guitarist Jonny Buckland and singer Chris Martin initially connected during their orientation week at University College London (UCL) in 1996. They decided to start a band because they both had a passion for music.

The band was quickly completed by Will Champion on drums and Guy Berryman on bass. The band was formerly known as "Starfish," but a mutual friend proposed that they change their name to "Coldplay." The bandmates juggled their academic responsibilities with their artistic aspirations, spending many hours writing songs, rehearsing, and performing at local venues.

Coldplay self-funded the release of their debut EP, "Safety," in 1998. They gained recognition and a tiny but devoted following thanks to the EP. As a result of their success, they were able to sign with

Chris Martin Biography..

Fierce Panda, an indie label, and release the song "Brothers & Sisters." The second EP by Coldplay, "The Blue Room," which Parlophone Records released in 1999, was the band's big break.

The music business took notice of the EP's popularity, which paved the way for their debut album, "Parachutes," and catapulted them into global renown. Coldplay's formation signalled the start of an amazing journey that would make them one of the world's biggest bands.

CHAPTER 5: BREAKTHROUGH WITH "PARACHUTES"

The commercial success of Coldplay's debut album, "Parachutes," in 2000 marked a turning point in the band's career. Chris Martin's outstanding performance and poignant lyrics made "Yellow," the album's lead single, an immediate hit. The song's soaring melody and authentic expressiveness resonated deeply with fans, propelling Coldplay to the top of the charts and bringing them into the spotlight on a global scale.

With its introspective lyrics and evocative soundscapes, Coldplay's album "Parachutes" showcased their unique blend of melodic pop and alternative rock. Songs like "Shiver," "Trouble," and "Don't Panic" that are melodramatic and extremely legible helped to solidify their image.

Chris Martin Biography..

Warmly received for its authenticity and inventiveness, "Parachutes" took home the Grammy for Best Alternative Music Album and brought Coldplay international attention. Due to the album's success, they won multiple prizes and gained a devoted following of fans all over the world.

It established a standard for Coldplay's subsequent records and laid the groundwork for their continued impact and development into one of the most recognisable acts of their time.

5a. Impact of the hit single "Yellow"

Coldplay's breakthrough song "Yellow," which is taken from their debut album "Parachutes," had a significant and wide-ranging effect. When "Yellow" was released in 2000, it soon gained popularity as an anthem among listeners all around the world. Here are a few salient features of its impact:

Chris Martin Biography..

1. **Commercial Success**: "Yellow" propelled Coldplay into mainstream success. It reached the top 10 in the UK Singles Chart and gained significant airplay on radio stations globally. Its popularity helped drive sales of the "Parachutes" album, contributing to its commercial success.

2. **Critical Acclaim**: The song received widespread critical acclaim for its emotional depth and Chris Martin's evocative vocals. Critics praised its simplicity and sincerity, which struck a chord with audiences looking for authentic and heartfelt music.

3. **Cultural Influence**: "Yellow" became a cultural touchstone, often associated with moments of introspection and nostalgia. Its melancholic yet hopeful lyrics resonated with listeners of all ages, making it a timeless piece in Coldplay's repertoire.

4. **Longevity**: Despite being released over two decades ago, "Yellow" remains a staple in Coldplay's

live performances and continues to attract new listeners. Its enduring popularity underscores its impact on music lovers around the world.

5. **Music Video**: Chris Martin's captivating performance of the song "Yellow" against the vivid yellow backdrop of a beach became a famous music video. It increased the song's emotional resonance and increased its level of popularity.

All things considered, "Yellow" not only signalled Coldplay's breakthrough but also proved they were a band capable of creating profoundly meaningful music that cuts across genres and age groups. Its influence is still felt today in the music business and beyond, firmly establishing Coldplay as one of the most important bands of the early 2000s.

CHAPTER 6: RISE TO FAME

Coldplay's long ascent to fame was aided by their distinctive sound, moving lyrics, and captivating voices. The following were pivotal moments in their evolution into one of the world's most beloved bands:

1. First Recording "Parachutes" (2000): Coldplay's first album was a critical and financial success thanks to singles like "Yellow." They won multiple awards, including a Grammy, and became well-known throughout the world thanks to the record.

2. **Successful Albums**: Following "Parachutes," Coldplay released several highly acclaimed albums that contributed to their continued success. Critics praised "X&Y" (2005), "A Rush of Blood to the Head" (2002), and "Viva la Vida or Death and All His Friends" (2008), all of which peaked at the top of major worldwide charts.

3. **Chart-Topping Singles**: Coldplay consistently produced chart-topping singles such as "Clocks," "Fix You," "Viva la Vida," and "Adventure of a Lifetime." These songs showcased their evolving musical style and ability to resonate with diverse audiences.

4. **Global Tours**: Their energetic and visually stunning live performances contributed significantly to their fame. Coldplay's world tours attracted millions of fans, solidifying their reputation as a must-see live act.

5. **Collaborations and Innovations**: Chris Martin's collaborations with artists like Rihanna and Beyoncé expanded their reach beyond traditional rock audiences. Coldplay also experimented with new sounds and visual concepts, keeping their music fresh and relevant.

6. **Charitable Work**: Beyond music, Coldplay's involvement in charitable causes, such as Oxfam

and the Global Citizen movement, further enhanced their global appeal and underscored their commitment to social issues.

7. **Legacy**: Coldplay's place in music history has been cemented by their ability to change without sacrificing their essential character. They keep putting out hit albums and serving as an inspiration to both fans and performers in the next generation.

The success of Coldplay can be attributed to their skill as musicians, their commitment to perfecting their art, and their capacity to emotionally engage listeners throughout the globe.

CHAPTER 7: CHRIS MARTIN'S MUSICAL STYLE

Chris Martin is renowned for his emotional depth, broad vocal range, and melodic sense. By combining pop, indie, and alternative rock elements, he has developed a distinctive sound as Coldplay's lead singer and primary songwriter. Crucial elements of Chris Martin's style include the following:

1. **Vocal Delivery**: Chris Martin's voice is often described as soulful and expressive. Listeners are deeply moved by his ability to communicate significant lyrics in an honest and transparent manner.

2. **Melodic Composition**: Martin is renowned for his ability to write memorable songs that linger in your memory. Songs like "Fix You," "The

Scientist," and "Yellow" show off his talent to craft strong, poignant choruses.

3. **Piano and Guitar**: Martin is proficient in both piano and guitar, often incorporating these instruments into Coldplay's compositions. His piano-driven ballads, such as "Clocks" and "Trouble," highlight his skillful playing and melodic arrangements.

4. **Emotional Themes**: Coldplay's music under Martin's direction often explores themes of love, loss, hope, and introspection. His lyrics delve into personal experiences and universal emotions, making their songs relatable and heartfelt.

5. **Evolution and Experimentation**: Over the years, Martin and Coldplay have evolved their sound, experimenting with electronic elements, orchestral arrangements, and diverse musical influences. This evolution keeps their music dynamic and relevant.

6. **Collaborations**: Martin's collaborations with other artists, such as Rihanna ("Princess of China") and The Chainsmokers ("Something Just Like This"), showcase his versatility and willingness to explore new musical territories.

7. **Live Performances**: Martin's captivating stage presence and upbeat delivery elevate Coldplay's songs during live performances, giving fans all over the world immersive and unforgettable concert experiences.

In addition to defining Coldplay's sound, Chris Martin's style of music highlights his abilities as a composer and performer. His ability to elicit strong feelings in listeners through music has cemented Coldplay's place among the most significant acts of their period.

7a. Songwriting and musical influences

The diverse range of musical genres and musicians that have greatly inspired Chris Martin's songwriting skills has shaped Coldplay's unique sound. Here's an overview of his songwriting process and main inspirations:

1. **Early Influences**: Because of his mother's influence as a music teacher, Martin was exposed to classical music as a child, which gave him a solid foundation in melody and composition. Additionally, musicians like Radiohead and The Beatles had a profound influence on his style.

2. **Lyricism**: Love, reflection, and resiliency are common themes in Martin's lyrics. He has a talent for writing songs that are both sensitive and approachable, evoking strong emotions in the listeners.

3. **Musical Diversity**: Coldplay's music draws from various genres, including alternative rock, pop, and electronic music. This eclectic blend allows Martin to experiment with different sounds and textures while maintaining a cohesive musical identity.

4. **Collaborative Process**: While Martin is the primary songwriter, Coldplay's collaborative dynamic allows each band member to contribute creatively. This approach enriches their music with diverse perspectives and musical ideas.

5. **Evolutionary Journey**: Throughout Coldplay's discography, Martin's songwriting has evolved from introspective ballads ("The Scientist," "Fix You") to more experimental and upbeat tracks ("Adventure of a Lifetime," "Higher Power"). This evolution reflects his growth as an artist and the band's willingness to innovate.

Chris Martin Biography..

6. **Social and Political Themes**: Martin's songwriting, which reflects his involvement with international events and humanitarian causes, occasionally touches on social and political concerns in addition to personal experiences. Coldplay's musical diversity and Chris Martin's ability to combine intimate narrative with universal themes have a lasting impact on listeners all across the world. One of the key reasons for Coldplay's ongoing success and impact in the music business is still his songwriting.

CHAPTER 8: COLLABORATIONS AND SIDE PROJECTS

Chris Martin, widely known as the lead singer of Coldplay, has collaborated and worked on a variety of side projects over his career. He has been able to experiment with different musical genres and work with a wide range of musicians thanks to his endeavours. Some notable side projects and cooperative partnerships with Chris Martin include the following:

1. **Collaborations with Other Artists: -** **Rihanna**: Chris Martin produced the song "Princess of China" from Coldplay's "Mylo Xyloto" album in collaboration with Rihanna. The song creates a dynamic and unforgettable duet by fusing Rihanna's pop vocals with Coldplay's rock sensibility.

   - **Beyoncé**: He worked with Beyoncé on the song "Hymn for the Weekend" from Coldplay's album "A Head Full of Dreams." The collaboration added a soulful and energetic dimension to the album's sound.

   - **The Chainsmokers**: Chris Martin teamed up with The Chainsmokers on the hit single "Something Just Like This." The song combines Coldplay's anthemic style with The Chainsmokers' electronic production, achieving widespread popularity.

2. **Solo and Charity Performances**:

   - Chris Martin has performed solo at various charity events and concerts, showcasing his versatility as a musician and his commitment to philanthropy. He has participated in global initiatives like the Global Citizen Festival, advocating for social causes through music.

3. **Film and TV Soundtracks**:

   - Chris Martin and Coldplay have contributed to several film and TV soundtracks, including "The Hunger Games: Catching Fire" with the song

Chris Martin Biography..

"Atlas" and "Game of Thrones: The Musical" for charity.

4. **Other Collaborations and Projects**:

  - Chris Martin has made guest appearances with artists like Noel Gallagher and Alicia Keys, demonstrating his willingness to collaborate across different genres and styles.

  - He has also participated in tribute concerts and special performances, honoring influential musicians and contributing to the music community.

These joint efforts and side projects demonstrate Chris Martin's versatility as a musician and his capacity to engage listeners with a range of musical endeavours. They enhance Coldplay's discography while giving Martin the freedom to experiment with fresh ideas outside of the band's parameters.

8a. Notable side projects and contributions

Chris Martin has dabbled in a number of side endeavours and made noteworthy contributions to numerous musical and humanitarian endeavours. These are a handful of the most noteworthy ones:

1. **Soundtracks for Film and Television**:
    - **"Atlas"** for *The Hunger Games: Catching Fire* Composed especially for the movie, this song demonstrates Martin's skill at writing music that enhances cinematic narrative.
    - **"Miracles"** for *Unbroken*: This inspirational track was created for Angelina Jolie's film, highlighting Martin's versatility in composing music for different genres.

2. **Collaborations with Other Artists**:
    - **Kanye West**: Chris Martin collaborated with Kanye West on the song "Homecoming" from West's album *Graduation*. Martin's melodic

chorus contrasts with West's rap verses, creating a unique blend of styles.

 - **Avicii**: Martin worked with the late DJ Avicii on the song "Heaven," which features Martin's distinct vocals and Avicii's signature electronic sound. This collaboration was released posthumously and became a touching tribute to Avicii.

3. **Live Aid and Charity Performances**:

 - **Live 8**: Chris Martin participated in the Live 8 concert series, aimed at raising awareness and funds for global poverty. His performance with Coldplay at this event underscored their commitment to humanitarian causes.

 - **One Love Manchester**: In the wake of the Manchester Arena bombing, Martin performed at the One Love Manchester benefit concert, supporting the victims and promoting unity through music.

4. **Tribute Performances**:

   - **"Life on Mars?" for David Bowie**: Martin performed a heartfelt rendition of David Bowie's "Life on Mars?" during a Coldplay concert, paying tribute to the legendary artist after his passing.

   - **"A Sky Full of Stars" with Peter Gabriel**: At the Global Citizen Festival, Martin collaborated with Peter Gabriel, blending their distinctive styles in a powerful live performance.

5. **Collaborations for Charity**:

   - **Band Aid 30**: Martin contributed to the Band Aid 30 project, a re-recording of "Do They Know It's Christmas?" to raise funds for the Ebola crisis in West Africa.

   - **War Child**: Martin has supported the War Child charity, which helps children affected by conflict. He has performed at benefit concerts and donated to this cause.

6. **Other Notable Contributions**:
  - **"Do They Know It's Christmas?"**: Martin participated in the 2004 Band Aid 20 project, a re-recording of the iconic charity single to raise funds for the Darfur crisis.
Global Citizen: Martin is a fervent supporter of the Global Citizen movement and has utilized his position to campaign for social justice, sustainability, and the reduction of poverty. He has performed at their festivals.

Chris Martin is passionate about music and dedicated to using his skill to change the world, as evidenced by his contributions and side ventures. His career has been enhanced by these pursuits, and his impact has grown outside of Coldplay.

CHAPTER 9: PERSONAL LIFE

As a global music icon, Chris Martin's personal life has often been revealed to the world. Some noteworthy aspects of his personal life are as follows:

1. **Family and Early Years**: Chris Martin was born on March 2, 1977, in Exeter, England. He is the oldest of the five children. His parents, Anthony Martin, an accountant, and Alison Martin, a music instructor, had a big influence on his early love of music.

2. **Marriage and Children**:

   - In 2003, Chris Martin married actress Gwyneth Paltrow. The couple has two children: a daughter, Apple Blythe Alison Martin, born in 2004, and a son, Moses Bruce Anthony Martin, born in 2006. Martin and Paltrow were known for their amicable co-parenting following their "conscious uncoupling" and subsequent divorce in 2014.

3. **Relationships**:

 - After his separation from Gwyneth Paltrow, Martin had notable relationships with actresses Jennifer Lawrence and Dakota Johnson. His relationship with Dakota Johnson, which began in 2017, has been relatively private but occasionally featured in the media.

4. **Philanthropy and Activism**:

 - Martin is deeply involved in various charitable causes. He supports organizations like Oxfam, Amnesty International, and the Global Citizen movement. His philanthropic efforts focus on issues such as poverty alleviation, human rights, and environmental sustainability.

5. **Personal Interests**:

 - Beyond music, Martin has a keen interest in yoga and meditation, which he has credited with helping him maintain balance and mental well-being. He is also an avid supporter of Arsenal Football Club.

6. **Privacy and Public Image**:

   - Despite his fame, Martin strives to keep his personal life private, especially regarding his children. He often avoids discussing his private matters in the media, focusing instead on his music and charitable work.

7. **Mental Health and Well-being**:

- Chris Martin has been transparent about his battles with depression and other mental health issues. He encourages people to get help when necessary and stresses the value of self-care and mental health awareness.

Chris Martin's personal life combines his charitable endeavours, family responsibilities, and music career. His commitment to upholding a constructive influence on the world via his music and humanitarian endeavours never ceases to motivate admirers and supporters across the globe.

9a. Parenthood and balancing career

Chris Martin has frequently discussed the challenges and benefits of balancing his demanding music career with his responsibilities as a father. Here are some specifics of how he manages to juggle his career and parenthood:

1. Prioritising Family Time: Despite his busy schedule, Chris Martin makes time for his kids, Apple and Moses, a top priority. He has emphasised the importance of being present in their lives through frequent activities or special family gatherings.

2. **Conscious Co-Parenting**: Martin and Gwyneth Paltrow have remained close co-parents after his "conscious uncoupling" from her in 2014. Both have made an effort to give their kids a secure and nurturing atmosphere.They frequently coordinate their schedules to ensure that one of them is always available for Apple and Moses.

3. **Involving Children in Music**:

- Martin has occasionally involved his children in his musical world, taking them on tour or to recording sessions when possible. This not only allows him to spend more time with them but also exposes them to his passion for music.

4. **Balancing Tours and Parenting**:

- Touring can be particularly challenging for a parent. Martin has addressed this by scheduling tours and recording sessions in a way that minimizes long absences from home. He also utilizes technology to stay connected with his children while on the road.

5. **Maintaining Privacy**:

- To protect his children's privacy, Martin keeps details about his family life out of the public eye as much as possible. He refrains from discussing his children extensively in interviews and ensures that their upbringing is as normal as possible despite his fame.

6. **Personal Well-being**:

- Martin practices yoga and meditation to maintain his mental and physical health, which helps him balance his career and personal life effectively. These practices allow him to manage stress and stay focused, both as a parent and a performer.

7. **Inspiration from Parenthood**:

- His role as a father has influenced his music. Songs like "Daddy" from Coldplay's album *Everyday Life* reflect his experiences and emotions related to parenthood. These songs resonate with many fans who share similar experiences.

8. **Setting an Example**:

Martin aspires to provide a good example for his kids, emphasising the value of hard work, kindness, and community service. His commitment to social causes and charitable activities is evidence of the principles he wants to instill in Apple and Moses.

Chris Martin takes a deliberate and committed approach to juggling fatherhood and his job. He juggles being a professional artist and a loving father by putting his family first, keeping lines of communication open, and taking care of himself.

CHAPTER 10: PHILANTHROPY AND ADVOCACY

Chris Martin is well-known not only for his music but also for his extensive humanitarian activities and support of several social causes. Some of the primary areas where he has made a substantial contribution are as follows: One of Martin's main organisers and performers at the Global Citizen Festival, which aims to end severe poverty by 2030, is

1. **Global Citizen.**
Martin is the curator of the Global Citizen movement and a well-known advocate for it. By uniting artists, activists, and world leaders, the festival raises money for worldwide causes and inspires social change.

2. **Oxfam:**
 - Martin has been actively involved with Oxfam, a global organization working to end poverty. He has

supported their Make Trade Fair campaign, advocating for fair trade practices and better conditions for farmers and workers in developing countries.

3. **War Child**:

  - Coldplay has supported War Child, a charity that helps children affected by conflict. Martin has performed at benefit concerts and helped raise awareness and funds to provide education, protection, and support for these vulnerable children.

4. **Amnesty International**:

  - Martin and Coldplay have been long-time supporters of Amnesty International, advocating for human rights and justice worldwide. Their involvement has included promoting Amnesty's campaigns and participating in charity events.

5. **Environmental Causes**:

- Martin is passionate about environmental sustainability. Coldplay has taken measures to reduce their carbon footprint, such as committing to a more eco-friendly tour and supporting initiatives that combat climate change.

6. **Red Nose Day**:

- Martin has participated in Red Nose Day, a campaign to end child poverty, by appearing in comedic sketches and performances to raise funds and awareness for the cause.

7. **Hurricane Sandy Relief Concert**:

- Martin performed at the 12-12-12 Concert for Sandy Relief, raising funds for the victims of Hurricane Sandy. His participation helped generate significant support for the affected communities.

8. **Love Button Global Movement**:

- Martin is a supporter of the Love Button Global Movement, which promotes acts of kindness and compassion. He often wears the Love Button logo during performances to raise awareness and encourage positive actions.

9. **COVID-19 Relief Efforts**:

   - During the COVID-19 pandemic, Martin participated in virtual benefit concerts, such as Global Citizen's "Together at Home" series, to support frontline workers and those affected by the pandemic. He used his platform to spread messages of hope and solidarity.

10. **Fundraising and Donations**:

   - Martin has been involved in various fundraising initiatives, including charity auctions and benefit concerts. He has donated significant amounts to different causes, demonstrating his commitment to making a positive impact.

Chris Martin's philanthropy and advocacy work reflect his dedication to using his influence and resources for the greater good. His efforts have inspired many fans and fellow artists to get involved in social causes, amplifying the impact of his charitable initiatives.

11. **Recent Work and Future Plans**

Chris Martin and Coldplay have remained active and innovative in their recent work, continuing to evolve their sound and engage with their audience in new ways. Here's an overview of their recent activities and what lies ahead:

Recent Work

1. **Album Releases**:
   - **"Music of the Spheres" (2021)**: This album saw Coldplay collaborating with artists like BTS and Selena Gomez. It features a blend of pop, rock, and electronic music, exploring themes of the cosmos and human connection. The hit single "My Universe" with BTS received widespread acclaim.
   - **"Everyday Life" (2019)**: A double album with two halves, "Sunrise" and "Sunset," it addresses themes of social justice, love, and the

human condition. The album includes songs like "Orphans" and "Daddy" and showcases the band's diverse musical influences.

2. **Live Performances and Tours**:
   - Coldplay has adapted to the changing landscape of live music by incorporating virtual performances and live-streamed concerts. Their innovative use of technology during the COVID-19 pandemic included performances like the "Together At Home" series.
   - The "Music of the Spheres World Tour," which began in 2022, emphasized sustainability, featuring eco-friendly initiatives like kinetic floors and energy-harvesting bicycles to power the shows.

3. **Collaborations**:
   - Besides their high-profile collaboration with BTS, Coldplay continues to work with various artists across genres, blending their distinctive sound with new influences.
4. **Charity and Advocacy**:

- Martin and Coldplay have continued their charitable efforts, supporting causes like global health, education, and climate action. They remain active in the Global Citizen movement and other philanthropic initiatives.

Future Plans
1. **New Music**:
   - Coldplay has hinted at continuing to explore innovative concepts in their music. They are known for their thematic albums, and fans anticipate further creative projects that push musical boundaries.

2. **Upcoming Tours**:
   - Following the success of the "Music of the Spheres World Tour," Coldplay is likely to announce new tour dates, with a continued focus on sustainability and reducing their environmental impact.

3. **Collaborations and Experimentation**:

- Martin has expressed interest in continuing to collaborate with artists from diverse genres, potentially leading to unique and unexpected musical projects.

4. **Social and Environmental Initiatives**:
   - Coldplay's commitment to sustainability is expected to grow. They may introduce more innovative practices in their tours and recording processes to minimize their carbon footprint.

5. **Film and Media**:
- It's possible that Coldplay may get into more media and movies, maybe creating special projects or soundtracks that relate to their musical themes.

Recent projects and upcoming endeavours by Chris Martin and Coldplay show how they are constantly growing as musicians and how dedicated they are to using music and activism to change the world. More ground-breaking music, avant-garde performances, and significant contributions to international issues are in store for fans.

CHAPTER 11: LEGACY AND INFLUENCE

In addition to his music, Chris Martin is well-known for his substantial charitable work and support of a number of social concerns. The following are some of the main areas in which he has contributed significantly:

1. **World Resident**:

Martin has been a key organiser and performer at the Global Citizen Festival, which strives to abolish extreme poverty by 2030. Martin is a prominent supporter of the Global Citizen movement and serves as its curator. The festival inspires social change and mobilises funding for global causes by bringing together singers, activists, and international leaders.

2. **Oxfam**:

- Martin has been actively involved with Oxfam, a global organization working to end poverty. He has supported their Make Trade Fair campaign, advocating for fair trade practices and better conditions for farmers and workers in developing countries.

3. **War Child**:

  - Coldplay has supported War Child, a charity that helps children affected by conflict. Martin has performed at benefit concerts and helped raise awareness and funds to provide education, protection, and support for these vulnerable children.

4. **Amnesty International**:

  - Martin and Coldplay have been long-time supporters of Amnesty International, advocating for human rights and justice worldwide. Their involvement has included promoting Amnesty's campaigns and participating in charity events.

5. **Environmental Causes**:

  - Martin is passionate about environmental sustainability. Coldplay has taken measures to reduce their carbon footprint, such as committing to a more eco-friendly tour and supporting initiatives that combat climate change.

6. **Red Nose Day**:

   - Martin has participated in Red Nose Day, a campaign to end child poverty, by appearing in comedic sketches and performances to raise funds and awareness for the cause.

7. **Hurricane Sandy Relief Concert**:

   - Martin performed at the 12-12-12 Concert for Sandy Relief, raising funds for the victims of Hurricane Sandy. His participation helped generate significant support for the affected communities.

8. **Love Button Global Movement**:

   - Martin is a supporter of the Love Button Global Movement, which promotes acts of kindness and compassion. He often wears the Love Button logo during performances to raise awareness and encourage positive actions.

9. **COVID-19 Relief Efforts**:

- During the COVID-19 pandemic, Martin participated in virtual benefit concerts, such as Global Citizen's "Together at Home" series, to support frontline workers and those affected by the pandemic. He used his platform to spread messages of hope and solidarity.

10. **Fundraising and Donations**:

- Martin has participated in a number of fundraising events, such as benefit concerts and auctions. He has shown his dedication to having a beneficial influence by contributing large sums to a variety of causes.

Chris Martin is committed to leveraging his resources and influence for the benefit of society, as evidenced by his advocacy and philanthropic endeavours. His charity endeavours have been amplified by the fact that many fans and other artists have been motivated to get involved in social concerns by his efforts.

11a. Inspiring future generations

Future fans and musicians can draw a lot of inspiration from Chris Martin and Coldplay's path from modest beginnings to becoming worldwide icons. Here's how they stay influential and inspiring today: ### Musical Innovation and Creativity

1. **Pushing Boundaries**: - Coldplay's openness to experimenting with many genres and styles inspires young musicians to push boundaries and create. Their transition from alternative rock to pop, electronic, and even orchestral components demonstrates the need for flexibility and originality.
-
Records like "Viva la Vida" and "Music of the Spheres" demonstrate their willingness to take chances and reinvent their style, encouraging other musicians to strive for uniqueness and audacity in their work.

2. **Authentic Songwriting**:

   - Chris Martin's deeply personal and emotive lyrics resonate with listeners, encouraging aspiring songwriters to draw from their own experiences and emotions. Songs like "Fix You" and "The Scientist" are celebrated for their vulnerability and sincerity.

   - The universal themes in Coldplay's music, such as love, loss, and hope, inspire future musicians to connect with audiences on a profound emotional level.

Social Responsibility and Activism

1. **Using Fame for Good**:

   - Martin and Coldplay's active involvement in charitable efforts demonstrates the importance of using one's platform to effect positive change. Their work with organizations like Global Citizen, Oxfam, and various environmental causes sets a powerful example.

   - Their commitment to sustainability, especially in their touring practices, inspires artists to consider the environmental impact of their work and adopt more eco-friendly measures.

2. **Mental Health Advocacy**:
   - Chris Martin's openness about his mental health struggles promotes a culture of transparency and support within the music industry. His candid discussions help destigmatize mental health issues and encourage others to seek help and prioritize their well-being.

Inspirational Career Journey
1. **Persistence and Dedication**:
   - Coldplay's rise to fame is a testament to the power of persistence and dedication. Their journey from playing small gigs to headlining stadiums worldwide shows aspiring musicians the value of hard work and perseverance.
   - The band's consistent output and evolution over two decades demonstrate the importance of resilience and continuous growth in a successful career.

2. **Balancing Personal and Professional Life**:

  - Martin's efforts to balance his career with his responsibilities as a father highlight the importance of maintaining a healthy work-life balance. His ability to manage both personal and professional commitments serves as a model for achieving long-term success and well-being.

Mentorship and Support

1. **Collaborative Spirit**:

  - Coldplay's numerous collaborations with artists across genres underscore the value of mentorship and mutual support in the music community. These partnerships provide opportunities for emerging artists to learn and grow.

  - By working with both established and new talents, Coldplay fosters a spirit of inclusivity and mutual respect, encouraging a collaborative and supportive industry environment.

2. **Encouraging Young Artists**:

Chris Martin Biography..

- Martin's public support for young and emerging artists helps elevate new voices and provides them with broader exposure. His endorsements and collaborations offer valuable opportunities for growth and recognition.
- Coldplay's involvement in music festivals and charity events often includes platforms for up-and-coming artists, showcasing their talents to larger audiences.

Lasting Legacy
1. **Timeless Music**:
   - Coldplay's extensive and diverse discography provides a wealth of musical inspiration for future generations. Their ability to create timeless, relatable music ensures their influence will endure.
   - Aspiring musicians can learn from Coldplay's blend of lyrical depth, melodic richness, and innovative production techniques.

Chris Martin Biography..

2. **Cultural Impact**:
- The band inspires future generations to think internationally and produce music that crosses boundaries through its worldwide reach and cultural influence. Their capacity to bring people together via music is evidence of the ability of art to promote intercultural understanding.

Coldplay's dedication to environmental sustainability and social problems shows that music can be a potent force for good, encouraging musicians to use their voices for advocacy and action. The creative, compassionate, and ever-expanding legacy of Chris Martin and Coldplay provides a compelling model for coming generations.

They continue to inspire and have an influence on upcoming musicians and music enthusiasts with their influence on the music industry and their dedication to changing the world.

CHAPTER 12: CONCLUSION

Chris Martin and Coldplay's ascent from their early college years to their current position as global music superstars is evidence of the power of creativity, perseverance, and social responsibility. Their innovative sound, poignant lyrics, and groundbreaking live performances have left a lasting impact on the music industry. Their global fan base and relevance have been sustained by continual artistic development.

Beyond their musical achievements, Martin and Coldplay's commitment to using their platform for good is demonstrated by their involvement in activism and philanthropy. Their dedication to topics like poverty alleviation, human rights, and environmental sustainability provides a powerful example for future generations of artists and fans.

As they continue to develop and innovate, many more will undoubtedly be inspired by Coldplay's

Chris Martin Biography..

legacy of musical genius and societal significance. Their holistic approach is demonstrated by the band's efforts to support aspiring musicians, Chris Martin's openness about mental health, and their dedication to both their careers and personal life.

In essence, Chris Martin and Coldplay's story is about more than simply their music; it's also about their enduring influence and the good things they want to do in the world. Their inspirational tale inspires the next generation to pursue their goals, endure hardships, and use their talents to make a difference in the world.

Printed in Dunstable, United Kingdom

66691234R00037